Making a Bad Day Better

A Kid's Guide to Battling the Blahs

Written by
R. W. Alley

Illustrated by
R. W. Alley

x

One
Caring
Place

Abbey Press
St. Meinrad, IN 47577

For Max and Cassie, who are in all the Elf books
(although neither wear candles in their hats!)

Text © 2006 R.W. Alley
Illustrations © 2006 St. Meinrad Archabbey
Published by One Caring Place
Abbey Press
St. Meinrad, Indiana 47577

Library of Congress Catalog Number
2005910479

ISBN 0-87029-398-2

Printed in the United States of America

A Message to Parents, Teachers, and Other Caring Adults

You'd think that with all the organized sports and computer games, all the camps and television shows, all the books and movies available to them, today's children could never, ever, possibly be overcome by feelings of boredom. As any parent or caregiver knows, you'd be wrong.

Today's children are no different from yesterday's children (their parents) or old-time children (their grandparents). They're smart and curious, seemingly full of limitless energy. They can also be unsure of their feelings and don't always know how to ask for help in sorting them out.

Keep in mind that no one likes to feel bored. Often, it simply happens. It's how one chooses to respond that's the key. As adults, we have learned our own solutions to push aside boredom. It may be calling a friend or riding a bike. It may be picking up a book we've always wanted to read. In each case, ours are individual responses that we have learned from experience will work for us.

When your child complains of "being bored" or that something "is boring," try not to lecture or judge the child by your adult standards and experiences. Instead, ask a few questions. Ask the child to put into his or her own words what "bored" means. This may help the child gain a sense of control over these feelings. Sometimes, it's even possible to talk a feeling away; the child may come up with his or her own solution.

One of the most useful things an adult can teach a child is how to be alone with his or her own thoughts. Nothing needs to be turned on. Nothing needs to be organized. Learning to be one's own best friend is the key.

This book talks about the many ways a child may become "bored" and offers a few ways to overcome the feeling. Read this with your child as a starting point for talking about these feelings. Let your love for your child and his or her questions guide you the rest of the way.

—R. W. Alley

Nothing to Do

So you're bored. That's too bad. No one likes being bored. It's a crummy feeling.

Being bored is waiting for something to happen, but nothing happens. Nothing at all. And, worse, you feel like all this nothing is going to last forever.

Luckily, feeling bored is one of those feelings you can do something about. Feeling bored isn't a feeling that comes from outside you…it comes from inside. And while maybe you can't stop the feeling of being bored from starting, you can keep it from sticking around.

The first thing you have to ask is, "Why am I bored?"

Everything Around You

You get bored because you are a clever, thinking person, always trying to figure out new things. People are just built that way.

If you were a flower, understanding new things wouldn't matter. All that would matter would be finding water for your roots and sun for your leaves.

If you were a squirrel, you might have more on your mind. But, still, all squirrels do pretty much the same thing to find nuts and build homes in the trees. There's not much time left for understanding music or soccer.

But, you're curious about everything around you. You know there are things you want to find out more about. Sometimes, the things that interest you are hard to find. You wait for things to find you. That's when you become bored.

Everyone Gets Bored

Everyone, everywhere feels bored sometimes. There isn't one person who hasn't just plopped down on the ground and thought, "I have never been so bored."

But, you don't always feel bored in the same way. Sometimes, feeling bored may make you angry. You may feel mad at people who aren't bored. Other times, feeling bored may make you feel tired. All you can think to do is snooze…even though you're not sleepy.

Mostly, when you're bored it feels like *everyone* else has something to do and you're the only one with absolutely, positively NOTHING AT ALL TO DO.

"Where Is Everyone?"

So, what happened today to make you feel bored? Why are you lying on your bed, staring at the ceiling?

Maybe your friend is busy at soccer camp or busy practicing the trumpet. Maybe Mom is busy in the garden, painting a portrait of the petunias. Or Dad is busy in the shed, inventing an invention to keep squirrels out of the bird feeder.

Everyone is busy doing things that they like to do on their own. It doesn't mean they won't have time for you later. It just means that right now they want to do something by themselves.

Time for Something New

Now would be a great time to try something new on your own.

Is there something you've always wanted to try, but never had the time to start? What about that model kit from your last birthday, the one you never thought you'd have the time to put together?

Or maybe you wonder what's so great about painting. Your mom is good at it. But, maybe you wouldn't paint the garden at all. Maybe you think the trees by the road are more interesting. When you're done with your painting, show her what you mean.

"It Would Have Been Fun"

Sometimes, you feel bored when the thing that you'd planned to do just doesn't work out.

It should have been a sunny day. Last night, you made sure the picnic basket was packed. The beach chairs were ready to go. You put your favorite towel in the bag with a sand bucket and shovels. You even got up early and put on sunscreen all on your own.

But, wait. Was that thunder? The weatherman didn't say anything about thunder. Is that rain on the windows? Is that rain gurgling in the gutters?

This isn't the way it should have been.

Time for a New Plan

OK, so your plan hasn't worked out for today. That's just today. That's not forever.

Make a new plan for the next day, or next week. Start a list: Where have you always wanted to go? What have you always wanted to do? Write down everything.

Ever think about climbing a mountain? Or fishing in the creek down the road? Or eating ice cream in Paris? Or steering a submarine to the bottom of the ocean? Or having popcorn at the newest Dragonking movie?

Now look at your list. Maybe there's something on there that you can do right now.

"Do I Have to Be Here?"

Sometimes, you get bored when you have to be somewhere you really don't want to be.

You're at a wedding and don't know anyone. Maybe it's for people your mom or dad work with. And you had to get dressed up and the seats are hard and the service is long. Could it get more boring?

Well, take a look around at all those faces. Imagine names that might go with those faces. Imagine the things those names might do:

Look, that lady's named Sue and she rides a camel to the supermarket. And, let's name him Uncle Bob. His suspenders came undone as he was reaching up to change a candle and his pants fell down.

Time to Think of Others

Sometimes, you get bored when you have to be somewhere you really don't want to be and you even know the people there—like your little brother's piano recital.

He's playing "The Happy Huntsman." It lasts one minute. Even with mistakes. But you have to listen to 59 other students play their tunes. You're bored before the first kid starts a song.

But you know your little brother wants you there. Look how proud he is. Change your bored feelings to feelings of pride at how hard he's worked. And give yourself a pat on the back for helping make his special day even more special.

"Why Is Everyone So Happy?"

So, what happens when everyone else is having fun and you're not?

It's the amusement park! It's big! It's loud! Your friends are having a great time. But, to you, the park seems too big, too loud. The smells and heat make you feel funny in your tummy. You can't even think about the rides.

Your friends zip around on the rollercoaster. They wave their arms, spinning around in the teacups. They steer the bumper cars like maniacs. And, they keep getting in line to do it over and over again.

"Come on, it's fun!" they call. But you just sit on a bench, feeling bored.

Time to Let Friends Help

Why aren't you doing all that stuff? It looks fun. Could it be, you're not bored? Could it be, just maybe, you're a little too scared to try the rides?

Tell your friends. They may tease you at first, but that won't last. They'll do what they can to help. And, when they do, do what you can to help yourself. Don't try everything all at once. Ride one ride at a time. If you need the bench again, that's OK.

You don't have to be bored. You can think about what you just did and imagine what you'll do next.

"Shouldn't I Be Bored?"

There are times you might feel bored because you think you should be bored. How can this be? Well, has this ever happened to you...

You and your family are on vacation. Your parents say, "There's a neat historic site just down the road. The buildings there are hundreds of years old. Very important things happened here long ago."

You don't even know the name of the place, but you just know you won't like it. There will be maps with lots of small writing and small pictures of sour looking old people from hundreds of years ago. How boring!

Don't Leave Room for Boredom

Yup, there are old buildings everywhere. Everyone is talking about this house and that building and who lived there and what happened there. But, you're not listening. It's a good way to stay bored.

But you can't help but look around. Maybe you start to think, "I wonder what happened here and there and over in that field." Could it be that you're feeling bored just because you don't understand what's going on?

Ask your parents to explain what you're seeing. Imagine what the people who lived in this historic house must have been like. Imagine how different their life must have been from yours.

The more you know about something, the more questions you'll have about it. Questions are always good. There's no room for boredom when your head is full of questions.

ye old
pony ride

There's Always Something to Do

Feeling bored is more about how you look at things than about the things that are happening to you.

Everything in the world changes, every second of every day. Sometimes, changes are really hard to notice: like the brush of a breeze. Sometimes, changes are really big: like a baby suddenly coming into the world, changing everyone around her.

With all these changes happening, there are always chances to grab onto something new. Let it pull you along. See how far it takes you.

Being bored means waiting for something to happen. Don't wait! Reach out and grab on.

R.W. Alley has illustrated more than a hundred books for children, including the popular *Pearl and Wagner* and *Detective Dinosaur* books. He has both written and illustrated another half dozen other titles, and has illustrated all of Abbey's *Elf-help Therapy* books. This is the first *Elf-help Book for Kids* that he has both written and illustrated.

Mr. Alley lives in Barrington, Rhode Island, with his wife and two children. During the school year, he often visits local elementary school classrooms, to talk and draw about how words and pictures come together to become the books that the children read. He might try out a new story on a class. And he always listens very carefully to the children's suggestions. You can check out his work at his website: www.rwalley.com.